ANOTHER ONE FOR THE BOOKS

Donald Gorbach

ISBN:1977629288
ISBN-13: 978-1977629289

"DON'T JUST COUNT YOUR YEARS,
MAKE YOUR YEARS COUNT"

-GEORGE MEREDITH